STROKE OF INSIGHT

AN ENGINEER'S PERSPECTIVE

Hei Wai Chan, Ph.D.

A joint venture between Simon & Schuster (1924)
and Author Solutions (2007)

Archway Publishing books may be ordered through booksellers or by contacting:

Archway Publishing
1663 Liberty Drive
Bloomington, IN 47403
www.archwaypublishing.com
844-669-3957

ISBN: 978-1-6657-3782-1 (sc)
ISBN: 978-1-6657-3783-8 (e)

Library of Congress Control Number: 2023901679

Print information available on the last page.

Archway Publishing rev. date: 01/31/2023

CONTENTS

ACKNOWLEDGEMENTS

Thanks to MassHealth, I could afford to be a long-term patient at Spaulding Rehabilitation Hospital in Brighton.

Thanks to my wife, Aeri Moon, who was instrumental in my rehabilitation. She relocated to San Francisco in 2019 to care for our son in Berkeley.

Thanks to my son, Andrew Chan, who is pursuing a bachelor's degree in English at the University of California-Berkeley, and provided helpful suggestions.

Thanks to my friends, Vivian WuWong and Howard Wong (Milton), who provide constant support and encouragement.

Thanks to my friend, Hing Loi (New York City), for humoring my voluminous emails with prompt replies.

Thanks to the numerous visits from relatives, friends, and colleagues: Winnie Heung & Hei Kuen Chan, Charles O'Connell, John McCall MacBain, George Davitt, Ashley Lau & Aryong Moon & David Lau, Aeryung Moon & Jeff Kahn, Teresa & Louis Moon, Rosa & Mike Song, Gita Karle, Din Shih, Mark Robinson, Susan & Liong Goh, Chiong Lin, Susanne Pan, Cyndi Mark & ManChak Ng, Shirley Mark & Fred Ho, Lydia Lowe & Frank Mark, DJ WuWong, Jonathan WuWong, Victor Wu, John Wu, Mari Smith & Vicky Wu, Linda Asato, Jenny Wang & James Zi, Melissa Wong & Robert Chu, Richard Wei, Judy & Silvio Ho, Jerhsing & Pastor David Lee, QingGuan Jiang, Ted Henderson, Stephen Wade, Kara O'Leary, Susan Sclafani & Jimmy Walker, Antonio de la Serna, Cynthia & Jun Chen, Pastor Ben Wong, Pastor Peter Lee, Pastor David Um, John Wong, and Pastor Sang Peter Chin. They lifted my spirit.

INTRODUCTION

The book shifted from my experience as a stroke survivor in the early years of 2016-2019 to generation-defining events, such as the global coronavirus pandemic, the Russian invasion of Ukraine, and the midterm elections in the later years of 2020-2022. Rehabilitation in the later years was repetition, repetition, and repetition.

One in four (or eighty-three million) Americans will have a stroke in their lifetime, according to the Centers for Disease Control and Prevention (CDC). Of that, 18 percent, or fifteen million Americans, will die from a stroke, and 72 percent, or sixty million Americans, will live with a long-term disability. Most Americans know little about stroke, despite being the leading cause of long-term disability and the fifth leading cause of death after heart disease and cancer.

I am an Asian American, a naturalized U.S. citizen, educated at the Massachusetts Institute of Technology (MIT) with a bachelor of science, master of science, and doctor of philosophy. I worked as a managing director of investment and portfolio management at the family office of John McCall MacBain.

I was in excellent health so suffering a debilitating stroke was a surprise. However, I have learned to enjoy my early retirement, although I watch too much cable news.

My life in four appendices:
- Appendix A: Life Imitating Art
- Appendix B: 80-20
- Appendix C: Religion
- Appendix D: Time

My experience in three appendices:
- Appendix E: Chronology
- Appendix F: Portfolio Diversification
- Appendix G: Cryptocurrency

My post-stroke challenge in one appendix:
- Appendix H: Dysphagia

I encourage every stroke survivor to take recovery into their own hands. There is a disconnect between the profit motive of the insurance company and your desire for a full recovery.

The brain is incredibly plastic. When one part is damaged, another part takes over. Unfortunately, rewiring is measured not in months but in years.

ONE
DAY 0 (TGIF)

It was Friday, April 22, 2016, and I woke up around 6:00 a.m. without an alarm. I mentally ran through my to-do list.

I drove my son to the Milton Academy in Milton, arriving around 7:55 a.m., and made it back to my office in Boston across from the Seaport Hotel around 8:15 a.m. because of light traffic. I tuned in to Bloomberg TV to get the closing results of the Asian markets (twelve hours ahead) and the European markets (six hours ahead) before the opening bell for the U.S. market. The U.S. stock futures were pointing modestly higher. Still, trading was choppy throughout the day. The market closed with the Dow Jones Industrial Average (DJIA) posting a loss of 114 points, ending just below the 18,000 support level weighted down by poor showings from Traveler and Verizon.

I stopped by George Davitt's office to discuss the U.S. market, particularly the DJIA. As usual, our conversation drifted to our respective sons, and we lamented how they had squandered their privileged education at two of the most prestigious New England private schools: Noble & Greenough School and Milton Academy.

I left my office around 5:00 p.m. As I drove toward the garage exit, I turned to the right to check for incoming traffic. Suddenly the garage appeared to be spinning, and I quickly pulled my car aside, followed by a wave of cold sweat. Sensing that I might need assistance, the garage attendants approach my vehicle. One even offered me a cup of water. Fearing a heart attack, I instructed a garage attendant to call an ambulance. An ambulance arrived within five minutes, and I was rushed to the Tufts Medical Center well within the golden hour. Tufts is designated a Level 1 Trauma Center in Massachusetts.

Upon arrival at Tufts, a resident physician determined that I had suffered a brain attack (not a heart attack) from severing the left carotid arteries in my neck. The standard treatment is to administer a tissue plasminogen activator (TPA). However, I exhibited high blood pressure (BP), so the doctor administered BP medicine first. I drifted in and out of consciousness. I recalled seeing my wife and son, peeing in my pants, and getting magnetic resonance imaging (MRI).

I wondered from time to time, *What if I was rushed to Massachusetts General Hospital instead?* Perhaps the surgeons at the Massachusetts General Hospital (MGH) would have performed a more timely procedure for my ischemic stroke, maybe a carotid angioplasty to unclog the arteries and redirect the blood flow instead of waiting to lower my BP before administering TPA.

Jeffrey L. Saver published a review paper in the *Journal of the American Heart Association* in 2006 titled *Time is Brain—Quantified*. He noted that "every minute in which a large vessel ischemic stroke is untreated, the average patient loses 1.9 million neurons, 13.8 billion synapses, and 12 km (7 miles) of atonal fibers. Each hour in which treatment fails, the brain loses as many neurons as it does in almost 3.6 years of normal aging."

TWO
DAY 1 & 2 (TIME IS BRAIN)

Saturday (April 23) and Sunday (April 24) were a blur for me, drifting in and out of consciousness. I recalled waking up in the elevator to get an MRI. I was told later that TPA was administered late Friday night (April 22). However, I was unsure if there was any causality from the TPA. I later experienced breeding around my frontal lobe. Instead of getting emergency surgery to relieve the pressure, I was supervised until Monday morning (April 25).

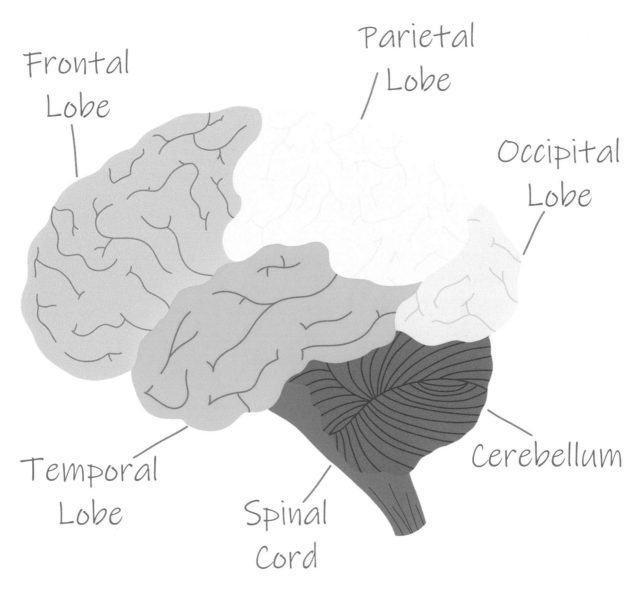

THREE
DAY 3 (ALIVE)

The opened skull surgery on Monday morning (April 25) was a success. Unfortunately, there was significant damage to my brain.

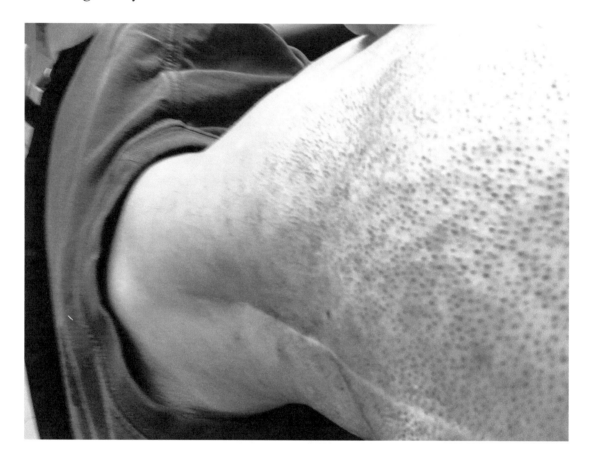

By day three, I was on a ventilator to assist with breathing and a gastrostomy tube for feeding. Teetering on the brink of death, I was bedridden with right-side paralysis and communicated by blinking my eyes.

According to the CDC, strokes kill over 140,000 people yearly and are the leading cause of severe and long-term disability. On average, someone in the US has a stroke every forty seconds. Each year, approximately 795,000 people suffer a stroke. About 610,000 of these are first attacks, and 185,000 are recurrent attacks.

Around 18 percent (one in six) of stroke victims die from their stroke, 10 percent (one in ten) will recover fully, and 62 percent (two in three) live at home with lifetime disabilities. Another 10 percent (one in ten) require long-term nursing care. Much of the "spontaneous" recoveries will occur in the first three months, with "likely" recoveries over the following months. To facilitate brain rewiring, it will take years of rehab and repetitive exercises to stimulate neural plasticity.

I essentially suffered two back-to-back strokes: an ischemic stroke on April 22, around the back of my brain, followed by a hemorrhage stroke over the weekend of April 23, around the top of my brain, as detailed below:

- Ischemic stroke occurs due to an obstructing blood vessel supplying blood to the brain.

  - For me, it affected the cerebellum (under the cerebrum, over the brainstem) responsible for coordination, posture, and balance.

  - It partially affected the cerebrum (above the cerebellum) responsible for higher functions such as vision and fine movement control. Touch, speech, reasoning, emotions, and learning were unaffected.

  - It partially affected the brainstem (back of the brain) responsible for life-sustaining functions such as breathing and swallowing. Heart rate, body temperature, wake and sleep cycles, digestion, sneezing, coughing, and vomiting were unaffected.

- Hemorrhagic stroke occurs when a weakened blood vessel ruptures.

  - For me, it affected the premotor cortex (in front of M1), responsible for sensory guidance of movement and control of the more proximal muscles and trunk muscles of the body.

  - It partially affected M1 (frontal lobe), the primary motor cortex responsible for motor functions such as talking and walking. Intelligence, concentration, self-awareness, speaking, writing, judgment, planning, problem-solving, and personality were unaffected.

FOUR
DAY 4 TO 7 (NOT MY TIME)

My younger brother (Hei Kuen Chan) and his wife flew from Hong Kong to visit me at Tufts's Recovery Room. We settled on a system of "yes," which was signaled with one long blink and "no" with two short blinks of my eyes. They proceeded to read to me the daily financial news and current events.

My wife visited daily and worked tirelessly behind the scene to have me transferred to MGH. Tufts agreed to discharge me once I was in stable condition.

I tired quickly and drifted to sleep often. I occasionally woke as the nurse, and certified nursing assistant (CNA) turned me in bed from side to side to prevent bedsores. I recalled getting a chest PT periodically to loosen the phlegm in my lungs.

I had some of the weirdest dreams, perhaps drug-induced hallucinations. I learned later that general anesthesia during surgery could cause temporary memory loss.

I dreamed of lost time, teetering on a knife-edge between life and death, where I, for a nanosecond, was teleported to the Vatican. I spoke with an assistant to the pope, who told me that it was not my time and that I would recover entirely but that the road to full recovery would be long and arduous.

Another couple was involved in a car accident after the male driver suffered a stroke. They, too, were rushed to Tufts's Trauma Center. The male driver miraculously recovered and took care of his affairs, only to die shortly after, just as foretold by the pope's assistant.

Finally, I was assigned to lead a squadron of "good" insectoids to rid the world of "evil" insectoids preying on unsuspecting Christians. The effort took several days. Of course, I told no one for fear of being locked up in a mental institution.

FIVE
WEEK 2 (MGH)

By the end of week one, Tufts finally deemed me sufficiently stable medically to be transferred to MGH. However, MGH insisted I undergo another week of observations before clearing me to undergo acute rehabilitation (rehab).

I was still in a daze, although the nature of my dreams shifted from a holy warrior to a bedridden cripple determined to walk again.

I recalled being on the upper floor, undergoing rehab in a spa-like setting. Somehow I imagined rehab in a wheelchair, frolicking under a water fountain, which is far from true. The next day I was sent downstairs because I was not ready to begin rehab. I was evaluated by a rehab team consisting of an occupational therapist (OT), a physical therapist (PT), and a speech-language pathologist (SLP), and they tested me extensively on the extent of my neurological damage. I was asked the date, where I was, the sitting president, and short-term memory recall. My fingers, arms, and legs were tested for strength and motor control. I was introduced to a spelling board, which I readily mastered and spelled "rehab" in response to their question: *Is there anything you need?*

Since I remained bedridden, my principal's lawyer (Charles O'Connell) helped me execute a power of attorney and a medical proxy, empowering my wife to put my financial and medical affairs in order.

SIX
WEEK 3 TO MONTH 3 (MIRACLE)

Upon my wife's insistence, I was admitted to Spaulding Boston in Charlestown.

Charlestown is the flagship location of Spaulding, with state-of-art facilities designed with inputs from the nurses and therapists. Every room is a single room with a wall-to-wall window and a water view, a sofa, an en-suite bathroom with a shower, and a small in-room refrigerator. The rehab gym takes up half the second floor. There is an extensive array of adaptive equipment for sports, such as tennis, cycling, and rowing. There are counseling and support groups for returning stroke survivors who achieved full recovery after decades of rehab.

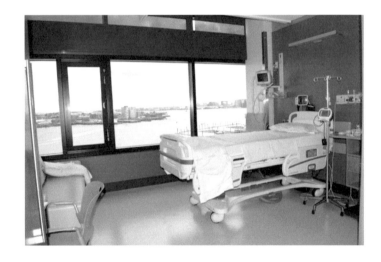

I received four hours of rehab five times a week, often starting at 9:00 a.m. The SLP was the first to discontinue my therapy after a modified barium test (MBT) showed that my swallowing function was severely compromised. The other therapists, OT and PT, often transferred me to and from a wheelchair with a hauling apparatus. I recalled peeing and shitting in bed in my diaper because I was bedridden with right-side paralysis. Nevertheless, the therapists were determined to prepare me to go home in three weeks. My wife fought with them to keep me in rehab longer, often enlisting outside review board to delay my discharge date several times.

Nevertheless, I was forced to leave Spaulding Boston in month three for Spaulding Cambridge. Although the facility at Spaulding Cambridge is dated, the caliber of the therapists is on par with those at Charlestown.

My wife frequently visited and, each time applied holy anointing oil to my right hand, arm, and leg, which later proved to be instrumental in restoring functions to my right side.

Around this time, there was a steady stream of visitors. First were friends from my college days. Then folks from my son's private high school. I was especially appreciative that my former colleague and principal visited. Of course, there was my former college roommate (Richard Wei) from MIT, who flew from Shanghai and sat next to me as I dozed off.

SEVEN
MONTH 4 TO 19 (DENIAL)

Rehab at Spaulding Cambridge (month four), NewBridge (Hebrew) in Dedham (months five to seven), Spaulding North End (months eight to seventeen), and Spaulding Brighton (months eighteen to present) was uneventful.

Changing facilities were dictated by insurance: our primary health insurance, Blue Cross Blue Shield, max-out after the first six months. On the advice of Spaulding Cambridge, I purchased supplemental CommonHealth insurance through MassHealth, which max-out after the next six months. For year two, based on the guidance of Spaulding North End, I hired an elderly-care lawyer to apply for long-term care under MassHealth. After extensive estate planning and documentation, I was eligible for Long-Term Care services under MassHealth. Essentially I have to be asset-less. I could use my retirement assets to pay down debts such as a mortgage.

In October 2017, Spaulding North End merged with Spaulding West Roxbury to become Spaulding Brighton (aka Spaulding Nursing and Therapy Center Brighton).

As a long-term patient at Spaulding Brighton, I witnessed first-hand the treatment of the residents in their 80s or 90s. Abandoned by their family and struggling with neurological diseases such as dementia, Alzheimer's, and Parkinson's, these elderly residents were easily irritated and often abusive toward the staff. As I rolled down the hall in my wheelchair, I could tell which room belonged to these residents by the stenches of urine emanating from the room. Nevertheless, Spaulding is ranked #2 in the nation by U.S. News & World Report.

As I got stronger week by week, these residents grew weaker. Most required a CNA to assist them in getting dressed and undressed, getting in and out of bed, going to and from their wheelchair, and using the toilet. Some needed a CNA to feed them and transport them from room to room.

Given that this center is their "home," numerous activities were available to challenge and entertain them mentally and physically from 10:00 a.m. to 7:00 p.m. every day. Activities included coffee & conversation, group stretches, arts & crafts, balloon sports, Bingo, dice or board games, trivia, book club, stories & poetry, concerts, karaoke, barn animals, cooking demonstrations, happy hours, and ice cream socials.

Being bedridden month after month, it would be easy to feel sorry for myself and ask: *Why me?*

My focus was to get better. I read up on stroke and recovery expectations. I understood that it would take time for my brain to heal. I was determined to make a full recovery. So the days rolled into a week, the weeks rolled into a month, and the months rolled into a year.

That said, I am in good spirits, so I didn't need anti-depression pills. I am pain-free, so I didn't need addictive painkillers. However, once non-prescription sales of recreational marijuana are legalized in Massachusetts, I would like to have a brownie laced with marijuana.

Oddly, I remember the day of my stroke (April 22, 2016) as if it was yesterday, while the years of rehab seem like a monotonous blur.

EIGHT
2018 (TRUTH OR DARE)

Some people can't handle the truth. They prefer to live blissfully in ignorance. Neither the healthcare professionals nor my wife was willing to tell me that I could be bedridden for life. I want the truth so that I can prepare.

On paper, I require 24/7 nursing care. However, I was determined to move to the other 10 percent bucket.

I decided to take all matters relating to my rehab into my own hands. I requested a change to my feeding schedule from overnight (2:00 p.m. to 10:00 a.m.) to daytime (8:00 a.m. to 8:00 p.m.). To facilitate this change, I sat in my wheelchair for sixteen hours (6:30 a.m. to 10:30 p.m.) instead of the previous four hours (10:00 a.m. to 2:00 p.m.).

Fortunately, my body tolerated this change.

I requested to increase my tube-feed rate (from 65 to 110 mL/hr) and formula concentration (from 1.5 to 2.0 Cal/mL). The ability to sleep flat took the pressure off my spine, which has stiffened over nineteen months of having to sleep elevated at 30° because of aspiration risk.

Furthermore, I requested my PT to clear me to get in and out of bed from my wheelchair without supervision. I also asked for clearance to use the toilet alone. After demonstrating safe transfers to three other PTs, my primary PT cleared me within a week. While this request was partially motivated by a desire to be independent, the lack of responsiveness from my CNA was a significant impetus.

At the same time, I requested my SLP to restart my swallowing trials of liquids and solids. My latest MBT showed nectar liquid was ingested, some pooling around my upper esophagus sprinter (UES), but no aspiration into my lungs. Nevertheless, the prognosis of this MBT was discouraging. I might not eat again.

Around mid-December 2017, my SLP started me with water thickened to a nectar consistency, then juices, sodas, coffee, and tea thickened to a nectar consistency. I progressed quickly in January 2018 to soft solids such as apple sauce, pudding, and ice cream. By February 2018, I swallowed puréed soup, puréed meats and vegetables, and chopped meats and vegetables. Of course, I relied heavily on techniques such as the head tilt to the left and chin tug since my swallowing muscles were not fully restored.

On February 9, 2018, I was cleared to consume thickened fluids, soft solids, and puréed foods independently.

On March 2, 2018, I was updated on the Food Service system to receive three "puréed" meals daily: breakfast, lunch, and dinner to consume independently.

On April 13, 2018, I was upgraded to consume chopped or grounded solids independently.

My weight has bottomed at 106 pounds (skin & bone). My pre-stroke weight was 143 pounds. At 5 feet 5 inches and over 55 years old, my ideal weight should be around 130 pounds.

Around April 2018 (month twenty-four), my former colleague (George Davitt) visited and advised my wife and me about colleges for our son (Andrew Chan). He agreed to speak with Andrew about the Stanley Park Scholarship (SPS) program. Andrew was admitted to the University of California-Berkeley with an estimated cost of attendance of $70,000 per year for an out-of-state student. An SPS of $60,000 a year would be a significant relief financially.

April 22, 2018, was the second anniversary of my stroke. That week, my former college classmate (Robert Chu), who was the head of the Melbourne office of Sullivan & Cromwell, came to visit with his wife on Tuesday (April 24) after his Harvard Law School reunion over the previous weekend (April 21 & 22) and an MIT conference on Monday (April 23).

On June 22, 2018, I had a Care Plan meeting, requested by my therapists (OT, PT, and SLP) and facilitated by the social worker (Julia Kingsley) at Spaulding Brighton.

The social worker reiterated that I was grandfathered as a long-term patient under MassHealth and subjected to periodic reviews for financial eligibility.

As for the therapists, they could justify rehab sessions for me until mid-July 2018.

On July 29, 2018, my weight was up to 120 pounds.

On August 6, 2018, I had a repeat procedure to dilate (using Botox) my UES to allow food to pass to my stomach. However, with my UES widened, there was an increased risk of acid reflux and aspiration. The last time I had this procedure was in February 2017. I developed aspiration pneumonia shortly afterward and was hospitalized for a week with IV antibiotics. This time, the same risk should be significantly lower because I am sitting up longer.

On August 6, 2018, one of the residents, an ex-marine, ex-Red Sox player, ex-agent for Lady GaGa, and ex-horse whisperer, passed away peacefully in the arms of his CNA. The official cause of death was heart failure. At ninety-five years old, he was survived by his ex-wife, daughter, and grandson. He received a military burial befitting a hero who had served his country faithfully.

On August 25, 2018, my good friend from high school (Antonio de la Serna) came to visit.

Being cognitively intact is both a blessing and a curse. I am constantly seeking new challenges to keep from losing my mind. I woke every morning wondering if I was living in an alternate universe where Donald Trump was the U.S. President and I was in a wheelchair.

NINE
2019 (COMMUNITY)

In early February, my wife relocated to San Francisco to be closer to our son, a sophomore at UC Berkeley.

I participated in eleven off-site activities, including a movie (Avengers: Endgame), a bank visit (Bank of America), an aquarium (Boston), and a noodle restaurant (Hokkaido Ramen Santouka).

On Tuesday, December 31, we had the first reported case of SARS-CoV-2 (aka COVID-19) in Wuhan, China.

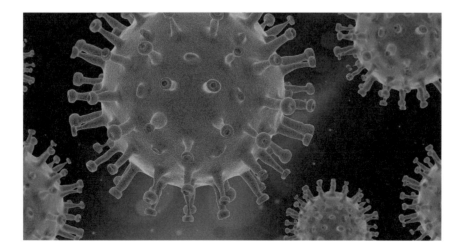

Given a human brain has over one hundred trillion neural connections joining together over one hundred billion neurons, 5 percent of brain damage from a stroke necessitates five trillion new neural connections. Therefore, neuroplasticity or rewiring the brain is a complex process that would take years. For comparison, there are a hundred billion stars in our Milky Way galaxy in a universe of two trillion galaxies.

The ensuing years were far from uneventful with the global coronavirus pandemic, and Trumpism as a political movement in the U.S. These events require a thorough treatment in separate books.

TEN
2020 (MASKING)

On Monday, January 20, the U.S. had the first confirmed case of COVID-19 in the state of Washington.

Thanks to the pandemic mismanagement of U.S. President Donald Trump, the U.S. was responsible for 20 percent of the COVID-19 cases and deaths globally, with only 4 percent of the world population.

For work, I engaged the Massachusetts Rehabilitation Commission for vocational rehabilitation. However, I was deemed too educated to flip hamburgers.

I hope to continue progressing toward a full recovery at one neural connection at a time.

Think Stephen Hawking (of Cambridge University) or Professor Xavier (of X-Men).

ELEVEN
2021 ("HANG MIKE PENCE")

On Wednesday, January 6, the "Stop the Steal" rally quickly turned into a violent insurrection at the U.S. Capitol. The last time the U.S. Capitol was breached was over 200 years ago by British troops.

On Monday, January 25, I received my second dose of the Pfizer COVID-19 vaccine.

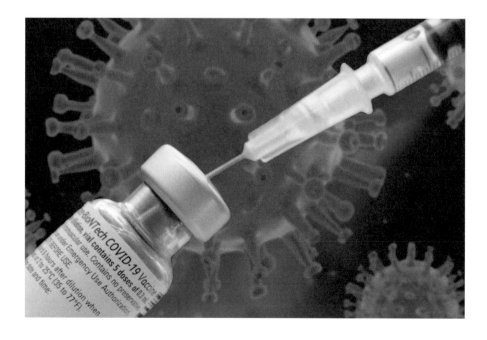

On Wednesday, October 13, I received my third dose (booster) of the Pfizer COVID-19 vaccine because half of my floor consisted of residents in their 80s.

As of December 31, the masterminds behind the January 6 insurrection remain free from accountability.

The "Big Lie" became the currency of the Republican Party because, quoting Mark Twain: "[A] lie can travel around the world and back again while the truth is lacing up its boots."

TWELVE
2022 (FREEDOM)

Ukraine

The disastrous Russian invasion of Ukraine and the fighting spirit of the Ukrainians will define 2022.

As of March 24 (four weeks into the invasion), 21,000 Russian soldiers were killed or wounded, and 6,100 Ukrainians were killed or injured, of which 3,100 were civilians (war crime).

In comparison, the 2014 Russian invasion of Ukraine and the annexation of Crimea resulted in six deaths.

Russia has been hit with unprecedented sanctions from the U.S. and European Union.

Houston

Thanks to my former high school classmate, Antonio de la Serna, who flew in from Virginia to accompany me to Houston, Texas.

During this weekend trip in August, I visited my parent's graves, attended a high school class reunion, and celebrated my 60th birthday.

In the picture to the right, we have Mayra Rosas (Passenger Support Specialist from TSA), me in a wheelchair, Dr. Ruth Smith (DMD), and Antonio de la Serna.

Midterms

Tim Michels: "Republicans will never lose another election in Wisconsin after I'm elected governor."

With the 2022 midterm elections around the corner, some Republican candidates publically stated that they would accept the election results only if they win.

Nearly 300 Republicans on the ballot in the 2022 midterms have disputed the 2020 election results.

As of October 3, 2022, Republicans controlled 54 percent of all state legislative seats nationally, while Democrats held 44 percent.

The conservative U.S. Supreme Court will take up a case from North Carolina that could upend federal elections by eliminating virtually all oversight of those elections by state courts.

The future of U.S. democracy was at stake in these midterm elections.

APPENDIX A: LIFE IMITATING ART

"I hear and I forget. I see and I remember. I do and I understand."
Confucius (551-479 BCE), a Chinese philosopher

"If I have seen further it is by standing on the shoulders of Giants."
Isaac Newton (1642-1726), a British physicist

"That's one small step for a man, one giant leap for mankind."
Neil Armstrong (1930-2012), an American astronaut

"To be, or not to be."
William Shakespeare (1564-1616), a British playwright

"The road to hell is paved with good intentions."
Saint Bernard of Clairvaux (1090-1153), a French monk

"First they came for the socialists, and I did not speak out—because I was not a socialist. Then they came for the trade unionists, and I did not speak out—because I was not a trade unionist. Then they came for the Jews, and I did not speak out—because I was not a Jew. Then they came for me—and there was no one left to speak for me."
Martin Niemöller (1892-1984), a German Lutheran pastor

APPENDIX B: 80-20

In business or life generally, the 80-20 rule applies.

By accomplishing 80 percent of the assignment in 20 percent of the allocated time, I have been deemed a hero.

However, the remaining 20 percent of the assignment often took up 80 percent of the time.

Of course, 80 percent of the deliverable must be directionally correct.

APPENDIX C: RELIGION

The tension between China-Taiwan is the highest in 40 years. Chinese President Xi Jinping announced reunification is only a matter of time. Taiwan President Tsai Ing-wen told CNN that China would invade Taiwan by 2025. The U.S. sold 5 billion USD of arms to Taiwan in 2020.

Would Taiwan be a flashpoint that ensnared the U.S., Japan, and Europe—leading to World War III?

In my 20s, I turned to political science for answers.

In my 50s, I look to religion for answers.

Higher-order

Whenever I think about God, I remember a physics example involving a sphere (3D object) and a plane (2D world) where D = dimensional.

When a sphere intersects a plane, it appears as a circle that varies as the sphere passes through the plane. From this, a 2D being could deduce the existence of a 3D sphere, but volume is not part of the experience of a 2D being.

According to John the Baptist, God interacts with man through his Son, Jesus, a man of flesh and blood.

APPENDIX D: TIME

As the playwright George Bernard Shaw (1856-1950) put it, "Youth is wasted on the young."

Before twenty, like most teenagers, I could not wait to grow up and be treated like an adult.

Then came work, family, and responsibilities. The years (the 20s, 30s, and 40s) just flew by in a blink.

Only in my 50s did I realize that the most precious commodity in the world is time.

APPENDIX E: CHRONOLOGY

HEI WAI CHAN

Mobile: 857-316-9652, E-mail: chanhw88@gmail.com

EXPERTISE

- Business development and leadership, financial technology and investment, credit analysis and risk management.

EXPERIENCE

Spaulding Rehabilitation Network, Boston & Cambridge & Brighton, MA   2016-present
Stroke Survivor
- Cognitive and linguistic functions are 100%.
- Fine motor control, balance, and swallowing functions remain compromised.

Aragain Capital Management, Boston, MA   2009-2017
Managing Director, Investment Management for the Family Office of John McCall MacBain (JMM)
- Responsible for tactical asset allocation, manager selection, financial investments and currency hedging on a billion dollars portfolio of alternative investments, real assets, equities and fixed income.
- Achieved wealth preservation with a global, multi-currency portfolio that generated an annualized alpha of 2.3% with a beta of 0.23 and annualized standard deviation of 7.9% (benchmark to 80% ACWI and 20% WGBI).

EdFinance, New York, NY   2007-2009
Co-Founder and Chief Financial Officer
- Secured $5 million in seed capital (from JMM) to establish a direct marketing platform to refinance private student loans entering into repayment. Returned $4.7 million because of illiquidity from the financial crisis.
- Secured $100 million in risk capital (from JMM) toward the leveraged financing of student loan auction rate securities.

Lehman Brothers, New York, NY   2004-2007
Senior Vice President, Securitized Products Group
- Targeted education finance companies with valuations ranging from $10 million to $25 billion.
- Led the acquisition of a private student loan company valued in excess of $100 million.

U.S. Department of Education, Washington, DC   2001-2004
Consultant, Office of the U.S. Deputy Secretary of Education
- Advised the U.S. Deputy Secretary of Education on disposition strategy for a $100 billion portfolio of federal direct student loans.
- Participated on an inter-agency task-force consisting of Office of Management and Budget, Treasury and Education to assess budgetary savings from loan sales to the private sector.

J.P. Morgan, New York, NY   1998-2001
Vice President and Head of Overlay Portfolio Management, Global Structured Finance and Credit Portfolio
- Established credit value-at-risk and economic capital frameworks for bank-wide exposure to credit and swap counter-party risks.
- Achieved $3 billion reduction in regulatory capital for bank-wide credit exposure using $40 billion of credit default swaps and synthetic securitization (BISTRO).

Union Bank of Switzerland, Zürich, CH and New York, NY   1993-1998
- *Director, Structured Finance Americas, New York, NY (1995-1998).* Co-started a Credit Risk Transfer Group. Executed over $11 billion in silent-unfunded risk participations.
- *Assistant Vice President, Global Corporate & Institutional Banking, Zürich, CH (1994).* Defined bank-wide methodologies for risk-adjusted pricing of credit; (RAROEC). Approved by the UBS Group Executive Board for implementation.
- *Business Analyst, Global Private Banking & Asset Management., Zürich, CH (1993).* Developed a business model for life-cycle investment funds and inter-temporal mass customization of asset allocation for private investors.

EDUCATION

Massachusetts Institute of Technology, Cambridge, MA   1981-1992
- Doctor of Philosophy, Electrical Engineering and Computer Science (EECS), February 1992
- Combined Bachelor of Science/Master of Science, EECS, June 1986 (Class of 1985)

High School for Engineering Professions, Houston, TX   1977-1981
- Valedictorian

APPENDIX F: PORTFOLIO DIVERSIFICATION

From 2009 to 2017, I was a managing director and portfolio manager for John McCall MacBain. I was responsible for a billion-dollar portfolio. The portfolio allocation was 75 percent in financial assets (diversified), 15 percent in business assets (concentrated), and 10 percent in cash equivalents (liquid).

Warren Buffets, the oracle of value investing, is quoted as saying: "Diversification may preserve wealth, but concentration builds wealth."

To diversify our financial investments, an endowment approach was taken similar to that of Yale University, Harvard University, and Massachusetts Institute of Technology. We invested in public equities, government and corporate bonds, hedge funds, private equity funds, venture capital funds, and commodities. To optimize performance, we would tactically tilt the portfolio, however, focusing on the selection of managers or stocks as a repeatable skill instead of timing the markets.

The business investments are concentrated and reflect the mission of the McCall MacBain Foundation: "[T]o improve the welfare of humanity by providing scholarships and other educational opportunities that nurture transformational leadership, and by investing in evidence-based strategies to address climate change, preserve our natural environment, and improve health outcomes."

The portfolio is managed across eighteen currencies to preserve purchasing power. We hold 5 percent in gold to hedge against inflation and currency devaluation.

APPENDIX G: CRYPTOCURRENCY

Tulip mania (1636-1637)

- At the height of the bubble, tulips sold for approximately 10,000 guilders each (equal to the value of a mansion on the Amsterdam Grand Canal).
- Tulip was first introduced to Holland in 1593.
- Fortunes were made and lost.

Bitcoin crash (2021-2022)

- As of May 16, 2022, 729 billion USD (or 56 percent) in Bitcoin (BTC) has been erased since November 2021.
- Bitcoin was first introduced in 2010 and had a choppy and volatile trading history.
- As an asset class, Bitcoin continues to evolve, and many factors influence its prices, such as becoming the national currency of El Salvador in November 2021.

In 2012, most investors thought bitcoin was a scam. Early adopters were criminal elements seeking to hide cash or secretly move money. A small minority believed Bitcoin was the future of currency.

In 2013, I considered investing $100,000 when BTC was trading at around 1,000 but opted not to invest because of a lack of underlying assets. However, even if I had invested, I would have set the stop-loss at 50 percent and sold my entire holding the following months when BTC traded below 500.

In 2018, I again considered investing in Bitcoin when BTC was trading at around 5,000 but opted not to. Never could I imagine BTC peaking at 68,991 in November 2021.

To be successful in high-volatility assets such as BTC, one must cast away any value-oriented investing and stop-loss discipline.

APPENDIX H: DYSPHAGIA

<u>Water [1] (December 2017)</u>
Water "Thick & Easy" (nectar consistency)
Water "Thick & Easy" (honey consistency)

<u>Juices & Liquids [1] (December 2017 - January 2028)</u>
Apple "Thick & Easy" (nectar consistency)
Orange "Thick & Easy" (nectar consistency)
Cranberry "Thick & Easy" (nectar consistency)
Grape (50/50 mixture with Water of honey consistency)
Pineapple (33/67 mixed with nectar Water)
Mango "Amazon" (33/67 mixed with nectar Water)
Green tea
Coffee with cream & sugar
Ginger ale
Pepsi diet
Mango smoothie "Naked"
Mango smoothie "Odwalla"
Tea "Lipton"
Hot chocolate "Dunkin"
White wine non-alcoholic
Lemonade "Minute Maid"
Beer non-alcoholic
Arnold Palmer "Honest Tea"
Electrolyte "Powerade" cherry
Red wine non-alcoholic
Root beer
Reduced-fat milk "Thick & Easy" (nectar consistency)

[1] Cleared (1/19/18) to consume "liquids" (thickened to nectar consistency) independently (without supervision).

<u>Soft Solid [2] (January - February 2018)</u>
Vanilla ice cream "Magic Cup" (melts into a pudding)
Apple sauce "Monarch"
Vanilla pudding "KozyShack"
Chocolate ice cream "Magic Cup"

Chocolate pudding "KozyShack"
Greek yogurt "Chobani" with pineapple bits
Greek yogurt "Chobani" with banana bits
Icelandic-style yogurt "Siggis" plain
Probiotic yogurt "Aptiva" with strawberry bits
Greek yogurt "Chobani" with orange bits
Greek yogurt "Fave" with honey
Greek yogurt "Chobani" plain
Cream of wheat cereal with honey
Whole milk yogurt "Dannon" with vanilla
Greek yogurt "Oikos" plain
French-style yogurt "Oui" with blueberry bits
Icelandic-style yogurt "Siggis" with peach
Greek yogurt "Chobani" with mixed berries
Greek yogurt "Chobani" with coffee
Icelandic-style yogurt "Siggis" with coconut
Greek yogurt "Oikos" with mixed berries
Greek yogurt "Oikos" with coffee
Yogurt "Yoplait" with strawberry-banana
Whole milk yogurt "Dannon" plain
Icelandic-style yogurt "Siggis" with vanilla
Greek yogurt "Chobani" with strawberry bits

[2] Cleared (2/04/18) to consume "soft solids" independently.

Puréed Soups [3] (January - February 2018)
Pasta e Fagioli
Pea
Corn chowder
Tomato Florentine
Squash
Chicken & rice
Clam chowder
Cream of broccoli
Minestrone
Ravioli in tomato sauce
Pea & mushroom
Cream of corn
Cream of tomato
Cream of mushroom
Cream of chicken
Chili

Cream of broccoli
Pasta Fazool
Chicken noodle
Cream of spinach

Puréed Vegetables [3] (February - March 2018)
Squash
Mashed potatoes with gravy
Carrot
Pea
Asparagus
Broccoli
Beet
Tomato
String beans
Avocado
Pumpkin
Spinach
Butternut squash

Puréed Meats [3] (February - March 2018)
Chicken
Hamburger patty
Fish
Spaghetti meatball
Breakfast egg (scrambled)
Meatloaf
Breakfast sausage
Breakfast ham
Hotdog
London broil
Corned beef
Turkey
Tuna
Smoked Canadian ham
Teriyaki chicken

Puréed Fruits [3] (February - March 2018)
Apricot
Cantaloupe
Apple
Pear

Pineapple

Puréed Bread/Pastry [3] (April 2018)
French toast
Blueberry muffin
Waffle
Bagel

[3] Cleared (2/09/18) to consume any "puréed solids" independently. They were upgraded (3/02/18) in the Food Services system to <u>three meals a day</u> of **puréed solids** to consume independently. Breakfast includes ham or sausage, scrambled egg, apple sauce, yogurt, and cream of wheat cereal. Lunch & dinner include meat, vegetable, soup, and fruit. Dinner includes, in addition, "Magic Cup" ice cream. All meals come with "Thick & Easy" juice or water.

Chopped/Grounded Solids [4] (April 2018 - present)
Hamburger patty
Cauliflower
Egg salad
Chicken salad
Chicken finger
Grounded beef
Carrot (soft cooked)
Turkey salad
Zucchini
Pear
Mixed fruits
Smoked Canadian ham
Corned beef with gravy
Lasagna
Broccoli (soft-cooked)
Breakfast sausage
Pork
Spinach
Tangerine
Apricot
Turkey
Snow pea
Custard pie
Pot roast
Pumpkin pie
Scallops
Peach

Dinner roll
Beef stir fry
Chicken stir fry
London boil
Chicken Caesar roll
Shepherd pie
Cheese ravioli
Soft boil flakey fish
Shrimp scampi & linguini
Beef stew
Stewed tomato
Baked chicken
Vegetable lasagna
Pork cutlet
Chicken Cacciatore
Pancake
Liver
Bacon
Stuffed shell (cheese)
Meat lasagna

[4] Upgraded (4/13/18) to consume **chopped/grounded solids** independently. Continue to receive three meals a day as before.

Printed in the United States
by Baker & Taylor Publisher Services